THREE GENERATIONS *of* POETRY

Mae Colgate Thompson
Esther Thompson Orlando
and
Bonnie Shaner Carniello

FITHIAN PRESS
Santa Barbara
1989

Dedicated to the memory of
my Grandmother, Mae Colgate Thompson,
who inspired my life . . .

Printed in the United States of America

Library of Congress Cataloging-in-Publication Data
Carniello, Bonnie Shaner 1943-
Three generations of poetry: poems by
Bonnie Shaner Carniello, Esther Thompson Orlando,
and May Colgate Thompson
ISBN 0-931832-19-5 (pbk.)
1. American poetry—women authors. 2. American
poetry—20th century. I Orlando, Esther Thompson.
II Thompson, Mae Cogate. III. Title.
IV Title: 3 generations of poetry.
PS589.C37 1989
811'.54'0809287—dc19 88-25181

Published by
FITHIAN PRESS
Post Office Box 1525
Santa Barbara, California 93102

CONTENTS

MAE COLGATE THOMPSON

A TALK WITH MYSELF

While strolling along and thinking one day
I met myself on a long highway.
I said to myself, "Pray, who are you?
How do you live and what can you do?
With life are you quite satisfied?
Have you ever your Master denied?
Do you visit the sick and distressed?
Have you shared the things you've possessed?
Do you pray for those who are needy?
Are you neglectful, are you greedy?
Has God ever said, *Come, follow me* ?
Did you stop and consider his plea?"
I answered these questions one by one
And counted the things I'd left undone.
My deeds, like ghosts seemed to stare at me.
I saw myself as I'd like to be;
And silently prayed for strength anew
To live for others and always be true.
I want to help others who've lost the way.
I've found my life is really worthwhile
Since I faced myself and talked awhile.

THE BABY TO BE

You'll love it just as much, if it's an ugly squeaking girl
Without a dimple or a single curl.
You'll love her if she's like the neighbors' brats
And just as mean,
Though her eyes be baby blue or lizard green.
If you should have a boy with freckles and red hair
You will think him perfect whether dark or fair.
Though he's as tall as Grandpa or handsome like his Dad
It won't matter much, he will be your little lad.
So it won't matter, if it's a boy or a girl.
To its Mother 'twill be the sweetest baby in the world.
If there should be times it will keep you up at night
You will insist to everyone, it is quite all right.

DUTCH BOY PAINT

If your house outside looks shabby and old
And the rooms inside seem cheerless and cold
I'll tell you something that will make it like new
The rooms will look brighter and cheerful, too.
Use a coat of paint called Little Dutch Boy,
Then invite your friends with pride and joy.
It costs so little and is worth so much
To give your house that homelike touch.

SAVE—SAVE—SAVE

Buy all the bonds you can
And put them on a shelf
This will help to win the war,
Then cash them in yourself.
Take all your old silk hose
And drop them in a bin.
All these many little things
Will help our allies win.
Prepare all your old tin cans,
Pile them in a stack.
It will give the enemy
Just another little smack.
Don't forget to write our boys,
It helps to make them smile
And gives them courage and strength
To run that last long mile.
It will take united effort from
Early morn till night
To wipe the smile off Hitler's face
And show him we are right.

FREE ADVICE

I once dreamed my neighbor was an owl
and lived up in a tree.
She came for a visit, looked around
then looked at me.
Free advice began to flow.
"Why don't you do this and that?"
"Why don't you paint the kitchen green
and give away that cat?"
"You should move the furniture,
it's not so grand this way.
Even though you have to put off your trip
until another day."
"I hear you are a widow,
you should find another man.
Of course, not too old or young,
just do the best you can."
I protested, people like to be themselves,
not like an ape who copies everybody he sees
of every size and shape.
How would you like me to come
and change your stuff about
and along with some other things,
throw your pet dog out?
My neighbor said, "I'm not a wise old owl,
but very foolish, I guess I'm nosy,
selfish, and often very muleish."
With this, she hung her head and flew across the street.
Then I woke up, smiled, and said,
"That dream is hard to beat."

BLACK DRAUGHT

I know a woman who was never gay
And had little to say
She nagged her husband
When he came in at night
Even the children she couldn't treat right
Her face was haggard and had a long look
She said her head was driving her crazy
Was listless and dull and awfully lazy.
Someone suggested she try taking Black Draught—
After taking a few doses, you should hear her laugh.
Her husband says she's a different woman
She looks much happier
And acts like a human.

LIFE IS A BOWL OF CHERRIES

Life is a bowl of cherries
If we can find the key
Which unlocks the door
That separates myself from me.
Once we find ourselves unselfish,
Fine, and true, we'll learn a lot
Of difference between the words *me* and *you.*
And if the cherries, which are days,
Are eaten one by one
There'll be no belly-aching at the setting of the sun.
Don't try to live tomorrow,
Just try to live today
And shed a lot of sunshine
And gladness on the way.
There is a joy in living
Some folks never find.
'Tis by unselfsh living
And always being kind.
So remember 'bout the cherries,
When the years shall come and go.
You'll find a joy in dying
Few mortals ever know.

MAYBE HE'S A FOOL

She dresses herself
In satins and silks
And is contented like a kitten
With a pan of milk.
He calls her cute names,
Like "my little powder puff"
When really she's nothing
But a great big bluff.
Her friends are amazed
And call her a freak.
But she says it's because
She uses technique.
She has hypnotized the man
I suppose.
Or else he's a fool
From his head to his toes.

TOO BUSY TO PRAY

Forgive me Lord, I am too busy now to pray.
There is so much before me, a long and tiresome day.
I know it's wrong to miss the beauty of the morning sun,
Perhaps I'll not take time to see its beauty
When the day is done.
I cannot listen to the prattle of the child across the street;
Or stop to say a kindly word to the folks I daily meet.
There is so much to do and time flies by on wings.
It leaves no time at all for simple little things.
Lord, forgive and help me find a way
To enjoy the world, be kind, and have time to pray.
At night I am too tired to stay awake and see the silver stars,
But restlessly I soar beyond nights' golden bars.
I slumber while the moonvine by my window is in bloom
In snowy whiteness, 'neath the summer moon.
I pray no more that my days with material things be blessed,
But for simple joys of life and quiet hours to rest.

IDEAL

I love your eyes so soft and brown
Your pleasant face without a frown
I love your understanding heart
To me you are God's counterpart.
You have been faithful through the years
And shared my joys and my tears.
You were always calm and sane
And have never caused me pain.
You are so fine, you should be real.
I'm glad you're mine, my ideal.

AIR CASTLES

Must I give up nor dare to dream
Because things are not what they seem?
Must I build no castles in the air
Cause critters say they are not there?
I build my castles wide and high
With towers reaching to the sky.
How dare you say they are not real,
They bring me joy, my life to fill
On days when life is very dark
Trials hover round me, cold and stark.
I build a castle bright and gay
It always drives the gloom away.

SIMPLE PRAYER

When just a child, I loved a little yellow bird
His songs, I still recall, the sweetest ever heard.
They cheered my lonely life
Helped banish childish care
And worth more to me than gold or jewels so rare.
One day he came, his little wing broken, crushed;
I knew he suffered so, his lovely song was hushed,
I prayed, "Dear God, please heal his broken wing,
For surely thou dost love each living thing.
I'd miss him, Lord," I prayed, "if he should go away,
But if it be thy will, I would not have him stay."
Time passed, I looked up in a tree and saw him there.
His wing was healed, his songs were gay,
God answers prayer!

PRAYER FOR MY ABSENT BABE

I'm thinking of you Bonnie dear, today
Hoping you are bright and gay.
May you never let life get you down
Nor your sweet face wear a frown.
Surely then, someday, you'll wear a crown.
May you travel through the years,
Smiling through your hurts and tears
Crushing out your silly fears
Always being gay
For this, I pray.

THINGS I LIKE

I like red roses and you,
Cabbage, potatoes, and stew,
Plenty of time and nothing to do.
I like new moons and silver stars,
Nice soft music and candy bars
I like boat rides late at night
And hours to sleep in broad daylight.
I like people, most any kind,
To be my friends, and peace of mind.
I like children, dirty or clean,
Good ones, bad, ugly or mean.
I like cold rain on my face,
Pretty clothes with dainty lace.
But of all things I like best
Is to be loved and sometimes kissed.
The world is full of many things
Enjoyed by paupers, peasants, and kings,
But of all the things I like best
Are friends whose friendship my life has blessed.

SHARE YOUR LOVE

If the many heartaches of our friends
We would seek to know
We'd be much gentler and sympathetic
Tears would flow.
But oh, how carelessly we crush the things they cherish so
And go lightly tripping on our way leaving spirits low.
If we would tell them that we care
Though all the world go wrong
And share with them a strength of heart
To make their spirit strong
If we would walk a mile with them
And let them join our song
We'd be repaid a thousand fold
With smiles, by friends who'd round us throng.

WHEN DEATH CALLS

I would not tarry a moment,
If death should beckon today.
I'd put aside life's playthings
And silently drift away
'Tis true I have work unfinished
And tasks that should be done
There are togs to mend, souls to save,
And honors to be won.
But I'd put all this aside
And willingly, cheerfully go.
If my Lord had not prepared for me,
He would have told me so.

NEVER GIVE UP

Once two little frogs, who had a lot to learn
While hopping around, hopped into a churn.
They swam and they kicked and floated about
But learned to their sorrow they couldn't get out.
The biggest and strongest croaked and he cried.
Finally gave up and peacefully died.
But the smallest kicked till he rested on butter,
Then croaked for help till along came his mudder!

TO A WOMAN

To be treated right, you should demand
Of him that he must understand
No smart woman, abuse will take
From any man for love's sweet sake.

CHURCH BELLS

Have you listened to the church bells
On a Sunday morn?
Saying to the children far and near
"Come on—Come on."
Oh, the beauty of the church bells
Calling you and me:
"Come and worship at my house,"
They call so tenderly.
Come on! Come on!
Children, obey the church bells now
Then when you are old
The sweetness of their music
Will linger in your soul
You will not want to stay at home
Any Sunday morn
When you hear the church bells
Calling you, "Come on, Come on."

THEN AND NOW

Once I craved such silly things
Like fur coats and diamond rings.
I let hours go by on wings,
Feeling often truly sad
Wishing for things I never had.
I couldn't see the roses round my door,
Or my baby smiling on the floor.
My busy mind refused to soar
Not needing anything at all.
I felt cheated, I now recall.
Time still flies by, the passing years
Have given me furs, diamonds and tears.
Now I'm older, wiser, death nears,
I crave today such simple things
Like the joy of a heart that sings.

A BIRD'S MELODIOUS SONG

Last night beneath the moon
I heard a birds's melodious song
It filled my heart with calm
That lasted all day long.
Today I marvel still, and wonder
Why he sang
Throughout the woods, across the hills
His lonely echos rang.
Lord, fill my life with cheerfulness
And let my songs be gay
That they may echo cross the world
To those whose skies are gray.

SPARE MY PRIDE

We sat so close together dear and
Yet so far apart.
You held my hand tonight and
Broke my heart.
You said your love was something of the past
Somehow I always knew it wouldn't last.
I've played a losing game with you and since I've lost
If I must pay the price, I'll smile at any cost.
Please never think of me as being cast away
For if your love has died, I would not have you stay.

UNPARDONABLE

You've come back with a tale of regret
Asking me to forgive and forget
Without a cause you slipped out on me
Asked for a divorce, I set you free.
When I was sick you left me alone
You said you hated to hear me groan.
I needed you then to hold my hand.
You went to the beach and played in the sand.
I was broke and needed a hat.
You spent your money for this and that.
I fell downstairs and broke my leg
Even for a doctor, I had to beg.
Now you've come back like a turtle dove.
Though you blighted my life and killed my love
I'm contented now and have good health.
You needn't tell me I'm sweet as honey.
I'm hard to fool, you want my money.
There's no hard feelings and good luck, Bill,
I hope you don't go where I think you will.

THE PATH OF LIFE

It wasn't easy along the way
I had so little time to play
Often my goal seemed far away
Yet I went on.
Sometimes there was a hidden flower
'Neath a dark and gloomy bower
And always an unseen power
So I went on.
I didn't travel alone all day,
Jesus went with me on the way.
I often stopped with him to pray
As I went on.
I've neared the end of a journey long
My heart is light and I sing a song
As I mingle with the busy throng.
I'm glad I went on.

ESTHER THOMPSON ORLANDO

THE DYING LAD

The campfire was burning on the plains that night
And a lad sat watching the beautiful sight
He was a poor cripple, but happy and gay
He had been growing thinner and thinner each day
His mind was drifting from the old campfire
To the shining stars in the dark blue sky
He was roused from his dreams by a soft, sweet voice
Her eyes were wet and her cheeks were moist
She was a beautiful lady, a sight to behold
She was his Mother, as I am told.
Her hair was dark, but turning white
Because of worry and the fight for life.
"Come," she said, "it's time for bed
And the day is long which you have led."
He turned and smiled, it was his last.
His breathing was slower, he was going fast.
He looked at the dying embers and said,
"We live not in vain, if we have been glad."

YOU AND THE SUNSET

I watched the sun sink in the west
And wondered which I loved the best.
I looked into your shining eyes
And then looked toward the darkening skies.
I wondered what the years would bring
Through the winter and the spring.
Would we be happy or would we be sad
Though the coming years be good or bad
Since the years are cruel, we'll probably part,
But I wonder if they'll change our hearts.
Your memories will help me to go on
Through bitter years of wind and storm.
The sunset in the skies above
Will help us always to keep our love.
We can be happy, no matter where we live
But if we grow bitter, dear God, forgive.

HOW AM I GOING TO KNOW?

How am I going to know you love me
How am I going to know you care
How am I going to know you love me
If those secrets you won't share
I'd be so lost if you left me
I wouldn't know where to go
So how will I ever find you
If you don't let me know?
If you ever meet that someone
You want to share your fate
You'd better tell her quickly
For you may lose her if you wait
So how am I going to know you love me
So how am I going to know you care
So how am I going to know you love me
If those secrets you won't share?

STORMY DEATH

Far, far away over the swaying trees,
Where the whippoorwills call in the morning breeze
A lad is thinking of the one and only,
For now she's left and he's awful lonely.
Can't someone help him and bring him cheer
Help him forget the one he holds dear.
He stands on God's stones and lifts his eyes
To the wailing winds and dark black skies.
He whispers her name down under his breath
And then a flashing light and then death
He can meet her now at heaven's gate
For the lightning has saved him from a far worse fate.

WAR

Brave were the men who won the war
Brave were the men who lost
But the bravest of all were the men who died,
Because of the life it cost.
Many ran through the enemy's lines
With explosives and bombs
To help save their fellow men
From the many enemy guns
When they were close near the lines
And could feel the heat
They never had even the slightest
Thought of retreat
Their loved ones at home were praying
For their victory
Why should they then wish to flee
The lines were not there, the men were soon within
By the help of God and those men, they could win
Why do men fuss and cause war to arise
While all around you some loved one dies.
Can't people see, there's no use for it all?
But maybe someday they'll be made to recall.

DON'T PITY ME

No pity please, I'm quite all right
My heart's not beyond repair
They've healed before in time to come
And mine's no worse for wear and tear
A broken arm is quick to heal
My heart will soon heal, too.
The scar will probably never show
And will soon be good as new
Please don't pity me at all
You should congratulate me instead.
By some miracle, I'm still alive
Though the heart in me is dead.
Give no thought to the wrong you've done
My heart's not completely cold
And through it all, no pity please
I still have my memories to hold.

PRIDE

The sun was bright as he said goodbye
And he smiled into my eyes
And I laughed, (a little loud) and joked
Oh, I was very wise!
He never saw the tears I hid
Beneath a gay outside;
He doesn't know, but he has my heart
And I, I have my pride.

I STILL LOVE YOU

I love the brooks that flow along
I love the birds that sing sweet songs
I love the trees and the flowers, too
But most of all, I love you.
You don't go away when winter comes
And snowflakes fly and raindrops hum
I love the flowers when they are here
But they go away when the snow draws near
The brooks may sparkle, the skies be blue
But it matters not, for I still love you
I have a question, I'd like to ask
It seems a hard and useless task
This is the question, ever how simple it may be
The words mean lots, "Do you love me?"
You may not answer, but if you do
Remember that I still love you.

TO MOTHER

Sunset on the prairies is a pretty sight to see
But the sweet look in your face is enough for me
The skies may grow cloudy and cold as can be
But the sweetest remains and belongs to me.

NOT NOW, MY LOVE

Someday I'll fall in love again
This, I'm sure, will be
But not now, my love, not now
My heart is still not free.
I will smile and look ahead
To the things I have to do
I will carry on, my love
but my heart will be with you.
The road ahead will be hard,
without you by my side.
Sometimes, I feel so helpless
and this, I cannot hide.
I have to push myself at times
to do the things I should
For now I have to stand alone
but you always said I could
I have my job and work to do
to help me through the day
and I have so many friends
who help along the way.
I'll not be sad and cry a lot
I know you'd not want me to,
though I know at times, I'll weaken,
I'll try to be strong for you.
Time will pass and I'll dream again
and my heart will someday care
but not now, my love, not now,
it's not my time to share.

MY HUSBAND, MY FRIEND

I'm glad we had at least some time
to talk before your death,
time to mend the fences
in the time that you had left.
When the doctors gave your sentence
of just a month or two
we were in a state of shock
and couldn't think what to do.
We talked a lot and cried a lot
and hugged each other near,
knowing the time was so short
made it very hard to bear.
We tried to make the time count
for every single minute
and fill up our every hour
with all we could put in it.
We did not dwell upon the future
of what we knew would be,
when he would have to leave this world
and there would be just me.
We had the time to share our love
and to show we really cared
and to apologize for past mistakes
of the life that we had shared.
We were thankful for the time we had
to let each other know
how much we really cared
and to let our feelings show.
We were both so glad we could say the words,
we knew we had to say
and we looked forward to
every short precious day.
We had time to make amends
and to talk out all the pain
we had time to say so much
and be best friends again.

TELL THEM NOW

Sometimes we fail to tell our loved ones
how much we really care
and someday we may be sorry
when they are no longer here.
We can't go back and right the wrong
when we have failed to say
some tender words or "thank you"
to someone we love today.
Life is so short and you can't go back
and tell them when it's too late,
that you have always loved them,
life does not always wait.
Show you care every second,
another chance you may not have
you'll be so thankful someday
of all the love you gave.
Don't wait until it's too late for you
to let them know how you feel.
You can't turn the clock around
and time you cannot steal.
Tell them today and you'll never regret
You didn't say what you needed to
and you'll never look back in sorrow
when time runs out on you.

MY FIRST BORN

I gave you the name of Bonnie
because I knew you'd always be
a bonnie little baby
and a great lady eventually.
You were my firstborn child
and the joy of life to me.
I was so very young then
and was happy as I could be.
We played with your dolls and toys
and laughed the days away.
We didn't need anyone else
to make it a happy day.
We didn't have a lot of people
with hours of time to spend
we were not just Mother and Daughter,
we were to each other a friend.
Now you are all grown up
with children of your own
and getting the kind of love from them
that you have always shown.
I know I can always call on you,
though you have your life to live,
I know you will always find the time
that I would need you to give.
You will always be Bonnie
with your eyes so big and blue
and you'll always be my daughter,
no matter what you do.

MY MIDDLE DAUGHTER

My little middle daughter
was so tiny and petite
she had a smile for everyone
that she should chance to meet.
She always had the biggest heart
and showed love to everyone.
She was such a happy child
full of life and fun.
She never sassed me back
if she did, I never knew
and she always did the things I asked
things she didn't want to do.
She's not just a daughter to me,
but a very special friend,
no matter what I want to do
she's with me to the end.
I always know if I need her,
she will run to be by my side,
and take me anywhere she goes
and show me off with pride.
She will always do the dirty jobs,
that no one else will do
and you can be sure that she
will always come smiling through.
I'm so glad that I had you,
my grown up middle child
and I'm always glad to see you
with your captivating smile!

MY YOUNGEST DAUGHTER

If I could make you happy again,
dear daughter of my heart
I'd do most anything I could for you
and I'll always take your part.
I wish I could take your pain from you
and make your sadness go away,
but just keep on smiling, Honey,
and things will change someday.
You haven't had it easy,
for one so young in years,
you've had a lot of hard knocks
and shed a lot of tears.
Life will be better for you some day
and these hurts will be the past
you'll soon find a new love
though it may not be your last.
You always look so happy,
with your beautiful smiling face
but your eyes belie the happy look,
though you try not to show a trace.
Contentment will come to you, I know
just relax and trust me, dear,
no one ever deserved it more,
out of nowhere it will appear.
Call me when you feel out of sorts
or need someone to talk with you,
maybe if you share your troubles
you won't feel quite so blue.
Remember, you are not alone
when you have someone to care.
Call me if you want me to listen
and you know I'll always be there.

MOM, I REALLY DO LOVE YOU

It's so easy for us to forget
how wonderful our Mothers are
and how they keep on forgiving us
when we push them much too far.
She's always there if we need her
to tell our troubles to
and she always tries to back us up
no matter what we do.
She might not always approve of
our choice of some of our friends
and might feel we're committing
an unusual amount of "sins,"
but when the chips are really down
and everyone is shoving you
your Mother will always be there
and keep on loving you.
One of these days, you may have
a daughter of your own
and you'll remember the love
your Mother has always shown
that's when you'll really know
how much Mom means to you
what a big heart she has
and how much she loves you too.
Take time out to talk to her
and show her you really care.
Let her know you'll try to do
a little more of your share.
Mothers, like Daughters, need to know
they're loved and cherished, too.
Take time out to hug and tell her,
Mom, I really do love you.

SMELL THE FLOWERS

Stop and smell the flowers
all along the way
for they may not always be there
every single day.
Stop and smell the flowers
just after the rain
for they may not be there
when you come back again.
Grab your share of sunshine
it's shining all around
Listen to the birds sing
it's such a beautiful sound.
Take time to see the beauty
of all things that are free.
There can be so much pleasure
in life if you let it be.
Enjoy life to the limit,
you're here just for a while.
You can't take anything with you
but you sure can take a smile!

I MISS YOU DARLING

I miss you darling, so very much
I miss your smile and your gentle touch
I miss you more as time goes by
for my love for you will never die.
We had a lot of good times and some bad,
but we made the most of what we had.
We made a lot of dreams come true
by working hard, but playing too.
We had a lot of years together
and waded through some stormy weather
We didn't always see eye to eye
and there were times, we didn't try.
There were bad times, that's for sure
but the good times made us endure.
It's very lonely, especially at night
when I go to bed and turn out the light.
I lie awake and remember your face
and remember the touch of your embrace.
We'll meet again some day, I know
when God decides my time to go,
meanwhile, I'll think of you each day
and dream some dreams along the way.

PASS THE SMILE

Happiness can come from a fleeting smile
that's given to you today
or it can come from a kindness you do
for someone along the way.
Have you ever had someone smile at you,
when you're feeling really low?
and all of a sudden you begin to feel
a happy kind of glow.
You can pass a smile along
to a man out on the street
and he can give it to someone else
he might happen to meet
If you frown and glare at others
it will make them unhappy too,
and if they frown at another man
that frown came from you.
If you walk with your head held high
and a smile upon your face
Just think of all the smiles you'll get
from the whole human race!

OUR CHILDHOOD

Come dream with me of the years gone by
of the sad, sad things that made us cry
and of all the beautiful happy things
with joy and pleasure that memory brings.
We didn't have money or a car to ride
or a big rich house to show off with pride.
But oh, we did have so much more
than some of our friends who were really poor.
We had a comfortable home with plenty to eat
and our clothes were always clean and neat.
We had friends both poor and rich
and we usually forgot which was which.
We all had dreams we'd make it someday,
but there were some who lost their way.
Our childhood was the best that it could be
with places to run and to climb a tree.
We had a Mother who loved us so
and she wasn't afraid to let us know.
She spoiled us all and equally too,
but would use the switch when she had to,
then she'd hug us tight and say
"Because I love you, I switched you today."
I could never understand how it was true
"It hurts me more than it hurts you."

PLAY ME A SONG

Play me a song of yesteryear,
the old songs are the best.
Play me a song I'd like to hear
they're better than all the rest.
I'll dreamily dance to a waltz or two
or whirl to a jazzy song
and cry a little at a sad adieu,
as I tearfully hum along.
Don't play me any of your rock and roll
or the smutty songs they write,
play me the tunes that soothe my soul
and lull me to sleep at night.
Some old songs will never die,
they will go on through the years.
They're part of all that's gone before,
they are songs of our laughter and tears.
Play me a song of yesteryear
with memories of the past.
Play me a song that brings a tear
those old songs will always last.

A DAUGHTER IS

A daughter is a daughter from the day of birth
To the day she breathes her last sigh
She's the hope her mother has in life
for a love that will never die
She's the one who will go on for her
and have children of her own
whom she will teach to show their love
as she has always shown
She will always forgive her mom
when she's not the perfect mother
She will stand against the world
That mom's better than any other
She always says her mother is
the best and the finest cook
and her mother is still so pretty
no matter how old she may look.
A daughter is a daughter from the day of birth
and makes sure that her mother knows
that she will always stand behind her
No matter how the battle goes.

BONNIE SHANER CARNIELLO

MAKE A RESERVATION FOR TWO

Make a reservation for two, my love
though I know not where or when
I'm coming to meet you
through forest and glen
The Lord will surely guide me
till it's time for us to meet
I'll stay here with our daughters
and pretend to be complete
I've loved you since I was near sixteen
when I was young and you were lean
We've shared a life and everything in it
It's hard to believe you could be gone in a minute
You were the reason I got out of bed
then into the night you suddenly fled
The Lord took you away without a fight
because we knew the time was right
Now I'm left behind like a seed out of sod
so make a reservation for two and then tell God
The new-fallen snow makes a blanket of white
and I wish you were with me to savor the night
to sit by the fire and hold my hand
to love me more than you loved the land
I'll try to be brave and do what's right
just know that I'm coming to meet you some night
Make a reservation for two and while I'm alive
I'll fend for myself and try to survive
I'll be there soon to join you dear
to spend eternity without any fear.

A LETTER TO AN ANGEL

Why did God take my love
and send him oh, so far above?
Why did he send me an angel and then,
take him away, not to descend?

I loved him with my heart and mind
and always will till the end of time.
No one knows, no one cares,
someone could ask, but no one dares.
Oh, if I only had my love,
I'd be so glad to go up above.

God, send me a sign and let me see,
that he was really meant for me.
I love him so and I always will,
he'll always be my one thrill.

Life seems to mean to little at times,
not even worth nickels or dimes.
He was so much a part of me,
did he ever really see?
He said, "I love you," on so many nights,
that I won't ever believe that God was right.

I know that I shouldn't question God's word,
for who am I— no more than a bird.
His kisses they thrilled me, his lips were so warm,
if I only knew he could come to no harm
I'd gladly give my heart, my soul,
if I might ever be so bold.

My love is not like a dying ember,
that comes in May and ends in December.
No, my love for him is warm and sweet
and I know in my heart, it'll never be beat.

Will we ever meet again?
Will he ever come and descend?
These things are not for us to ask,
just live with life, and learn your task.
You can't run away from life or the past,
but hold it close, cause it goes so fast.

Always lend a helping hand,
and stick close to our precious land.
Life is full of hardships, it's true,
but when you get to heaven, you'll see what's due.

Love one another as God loves you,
don't worry, my friend, he'll see you through,
God needed him so he took him to see
the beautiful land where someday we'll be.

Written 1958

SEAN ANNA

Sean Anna is my heart's delight
Sean Anna is a star so bright
She is a child so bright by day
so fair and young and wise and gay.
Children are such trusting things
to run to mom when the fire-bell rings.
They have such a bountiful lot of love,
like cooing birds or turtle doves.
They are a wonder night and day
to kneel at bedtime when they pray.
Seeing Sean grow each day,
it makes me think, when I kneel to pray.
If God wills it so and I have enough time,
I'll make for her a nursery rhyme.
I'll make for her buttons and bows
and lots of pretty frilly clothes.
I'll teach her how to be good and true
and to love others as God loves you.
Her dad can teach her how to catch a man
and I'll teach her how to hold him in her hand.
Childhood is such a wondrous thing,
it's so much nicer than a diamond ring.
It's so much finer than anything,
that I need the time, God, to teach her
all these things.

LITTLE TINY GIRL

Rani, Rani, how we love you.
Little tiny girl with eyes of blue.
You have your father's curly hair
and mommy's imagination to reach the air,
for dreams and cares that will come true
and days of happiness we've planned for you.
Little tiny girl so short and cute,
with a smile like angels or a song from a lute.
I want you to be such a loving child,
who's free and honest, but never wild.
God shine your light upon my love
and let her grow to be above,
the wars and battles we seem to see
and let her be a bit like me.
Let her heart with wonder, big and bright
be filled with only loving light.
Let her children, as we have now,
with eyes of blue and long brown hair.

MY LOVE

My love, my life, my sweetness and my joy;
how can all these things be wrapped up in one little boy?
Can time really erase the golden years?
The sorrowful heartaches and all the tears.
Time can make your thoughts grow weak,
but in keeping your heart strong, you'll hear it speak.
I've made an image of you , my love,
that nothing on earth could rise above.
I've worked and sweated to hold you near,
I've found that no one could be so dear.
If you found a home in a foreign land,
I'd hope and pray you would ask for my hand.
When life grows dreary, dull and gray,
I think of you to brighten my day.
I feel as a fox held at bay,
unless you're there at the end of my day.
Our being apart has crowded our love,
but made it stronger, as the wind to the dove.
Many a crisis we've passed so far,
but our hearts hold true without a mar.
If God wills it so and I get you back,
I promise there'll be nothing you'll lack,
whether in love, care, or emotion,
I'll always be giving all my devotion.
I'll never settle for being just a wife,
I'll also be your mistress the rest of your life.
In letting you know how much I care,
I think you know there's nothing I wouldn't dare.
God keep you safe, till you're home again.
May an angel guard you by being a friend.

HAPPY BIRTHDAY

You really are a sweetie and I really love you dear.
You are always in my thoughts, whether far or near.
This little note was written and formed the words to say,
Happy Birthday, darling, and I wish you the sweetest day.
I hope it brings you sunshine as that's what you bring to me.
To my heart you will always hold the key.
I know sometimes I holler and you don't think I care,
and sometimes I'm sure you don't think I'm very fair,
but I will always love you and I will always be there.

MY FAVORITE ST. PATRICK'S DAY

I met a little fellow out in the wood
He had red hair and a little green hood.
He didn't see me coming,
I snuck up from behind
He seemed to be staggering
and not following any line.
He hiccoughed and sneezed all over the place,
His nose and his eyes were as red as his face.
He seemed to be mumbling and talking to himself,
Then suddenly, I realized I was watching an elf.
All my life, I'd been waiting for my chance
to see a Leprachaun or an elf doing his dance.
People have said, "Well, I think she's crazy,
or maybe it's that she's smelled a rotten daisy."
But I know what I saw on that fair and sunny day
and if you get to Ireland, you may get your pay.
He finally found his tiny pot of gold
and I was right behind him as he leapt and danced and rolled.
I reached down and grabbed him
before he reached his cave,
and he had to give me what I always thought I craved.
At the end of my life, I have my pot of gold,
but the story's ending is glad to be told.
For more than the gold that lies on my shelves,
is the love that I've kept by believing in elves.

WICHITA BLUES

I've come so far from Wichita
to the top of the world you see
to be on my own, to run and roam
and see what I could be.
If I knew then what I know now
I wouldn't have strayed so far
from the place I love, the place that's home
the town called Wichita.
If I only had red ruby shoes
I wouldn't have these Wichita blues.
What I wouldn't give to walk the meadow
and the fields with sunsets bright and bold
to hold another in my arms to wipe away the cold
I hear like music in my ears
the train going up the track
and I know it's calling me
I've gotta be going back
back to the place where stars are bright
and shine all night and there's nothing in life I lack.
Wish I had those ruby shoes
to rid me of those Wichita blues.

MY GREAT IRISH PROTECTOR

I Have a great Irish protector
his name isn't O'Leary or Finn
But he watches over my shoulder
and spurs me to pick up my pen
When I am sad and lonely
and haven't anywhere to go
he lets me lean on him
and protects me from the foe
He reminds me that I'm Irish
and live in the land of the free
while Irish hearts are dying
far across the land and the sea
I have some nerve to fuss and complain
while Irish children can't live a life that's sane
A cheer to my Great Irish Protector
May God hold you close at hand
for it's you who
lifts my spirits
by keeping me out of the sand
I promise to try harder tomorrow
to remember from whence I came
to know all Irish are hearty
and all be proud of our name

THERE WILL BE THE WEARIN' OF THE GREEN

The most beautiful place in the world,
ravaged by Britain's Queen
God created a masterpiece and called it evergreen
I've never seen or heard the sound of Ireland's lovely shore
But I would go there if I could and stay for ever more.
I've spent my life being orange and green
and somewhere mostly in between
If England would only walk away and take with her the Queen
our lovely Ireland once more could live
and all the religions could remember how to give
They could remember all of life's traditions
instead of living in pure and whole perdition
It's really a wonder there are any Irish left
since the sounds of the guns have made them all quite deaf
To the beauty of the land and the shamrock pure
that the children who are born there are bright I'm sure
They should have the right to grow up unafraid
to walk without fear where the road has been laid.
Oh, would that I could free her from bondage and the fear
to let the children sing the songs and hold each other dear.
Heaven must have sides that gently overflow
for all the Irish who have died and seeds that cannot sow
On Judgment Day I expect to see the Wearin' of the Green
and no more fear for Ireland for there will be no Queen!

ONCE I KNEW A BUTTERFLY

Once I knew a butterfly, the most beautiful ever seen
He took my breath away, he was all purple and green
He stopped his flight for awhile and landed on a tree.
I sang him all the songs I knew and asked that he love only me
He stayed with me for awhile and all the time I was beguiled
He could not breathe our air
so he went away without a care
I gave him all I had to give
but he had to leave cause he couldn't live
Now I'm alone out in the wood
the song is quiet where he stood
Was it a dream, was he really there?
Can I go on without him, is that really fair?
The sun shines bright in the wood today
but the beauty's gone cause he could not stay
I'll walk on down that dusty road
trying to recapture the music that flowed
Maybe the magic he brought will teach me to be free
The memory of his beauty will live on through eternity.

WAKE UP, SWEET MISTI

Wake up, Sweet Misti, wake up from your bad dream.
The night is quickly falling, there's so much to be seen.
Your whole life is before you, now that you're seventeen.
Wake up from your nightmare
and find there's a world for you to glean.
You shine so brilliant, like stars that fall at night.
We know you can awaken if you try with all your might.
There's so much of life awaiting, there's things to see and do.
There's a reality of learning ready just for you.
We're all here waiting for you, just beyond the brutal light
Please muster up your courage and try to win the fight
Everyone is praying for the day you start anew
Your parents will stay by you, they're waiting for their cue.
We all have brought pictures of the ones you know
We all will treat you gently like softly falling snow.
Wake up, sweet Misti and rise like the morning star
We know you can do it, we know who you are!

MY FURRY FRIEND

We brought her home when she was eight weeks old
She was never bad and she was always bold
Her fur was white with silver ends
She'd wag her tail and romp for the lens.
She knew she was beautiful, so did the judges
She won trophies and ribbons and our hearts with her nudges.
She was my best friend and will be through the ages.
I have pictures and a scrapbook with many lovely pages
of shows and honors she had won
and all the years of having fun.
When the nights were cold, she'd warm our feet
She never really needed the heat
She read my thoughts and did what I'd ask
For her there was never too large a task.
When the children would fight she'd get in the way,
till they'd all start laughting and tell her to stay.
She had the most beautiful smile
and walked with me to the park for a mile
She never complained or got in the way
She'd stay by my feet most of the day.
When she left this world I held her tight
she just gave up, she'd lost her fight
I pray she's watching over the pearly gate
because she earned and deserved that fate.
I'll be there someday to see her again
God keep my wonderful furry friend.